Also by Gail Gibbons
Trucks
Locks & Keys
Clocks and How They Go

THE POST OFFICE BOOK
Mail and How It Moves
by Gail Gibbons
HarperCollins*Publishers*

POST OFFICE

To Parker Lange, Irene Ricker, and Gifford Sevene of the Corinth, Vermont Post Office, and to Doris Hipsher

Special thanks to Lionel Brochu, Michael Donahue, and Richard Wood of the White River Junction, Vermont Post Office

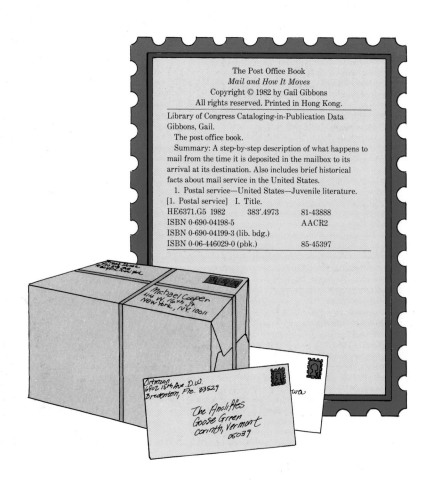

The Post Office Book
Mail and How It Moves
Copyright © 1982 by Gail Gibbons
All rights reserved. Printed in Hong Kong.

Library of Congress Cataloging-in-Publication Data
Gibbons, Gail.
  The post office book.
  Summary: A step-by-step description of what happens to
mail from the time it is deposited in the mailbox to
its arrival at its destination. Also includes brief historical
facts about mail service in the United States.
  1. Postal service—United States—Juvenile literature.
[1. Postal service] I. Title.
HE6371.G5 1982   383'.4973   81-43888
ISBN 0-690-04198-5   AACR2
ISBN 0-690-04199-3 (lib. bdg.)
ISBN 0-06-446029-0 (pbk.)   85-45397

Since early times people have sent messages and
packages to one another.

Nowadays we have modern ways of sending mail.

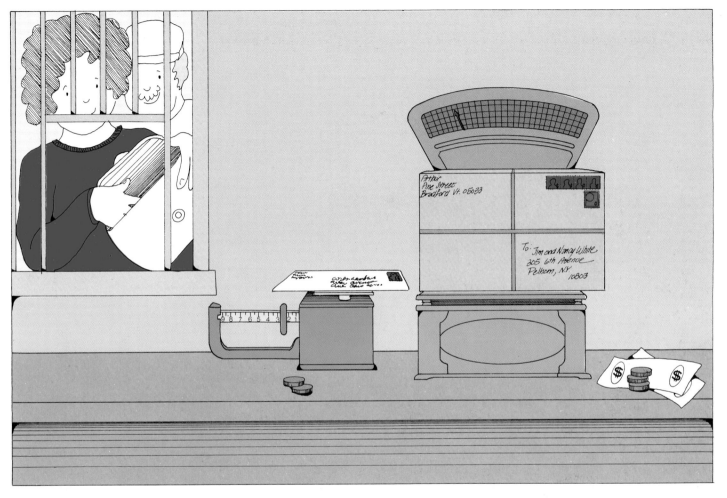

The sender pays to have something mailed. A stamp
shows the cost. A heavy piece of mail costs more to
send than a lighter piece.

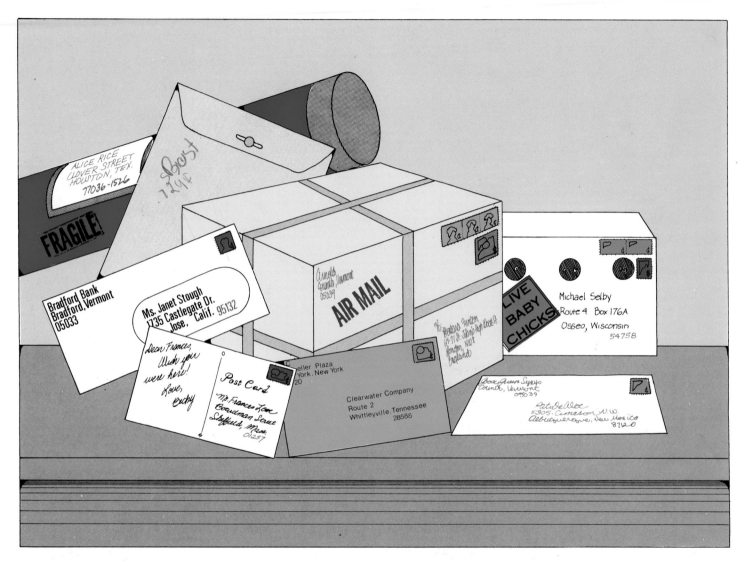

An address and zip code tell where the mail is going.

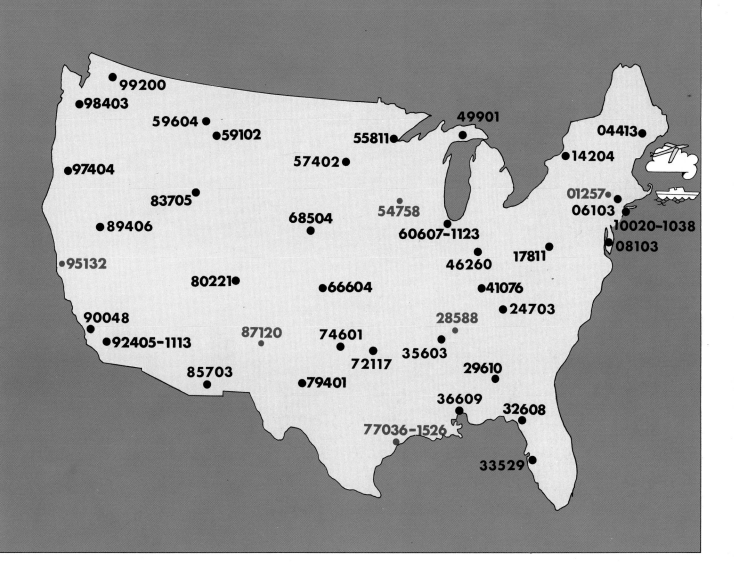

Things can be mailed at a post office

...or placed in a mailbox.

A letter carrier picks up mail from the mailbox.

The mail goes to the local post office, where it is sorted by hand to divide local mail (mail for nearby places) from mail for out-of-town.

The out-of-town mail is put on a truck

...and sent to the big area post office.

The big area post office receives mail from many local post offices.

Inside the big area post office a culling machine divides the oversized or odd-shaped mail from the regular mail.

Postal workers handle this mail separately.

The regular mail goes to a canceling machine.
The machine prints a postmark on the envelope and marks
the stamps with wavy lines so they cannot be used again.

Next come the sorting machines.

Postal workers at the machines read the zip codes
and punch the numbers into a computer

...which drops the letters into the correct zip code bins.

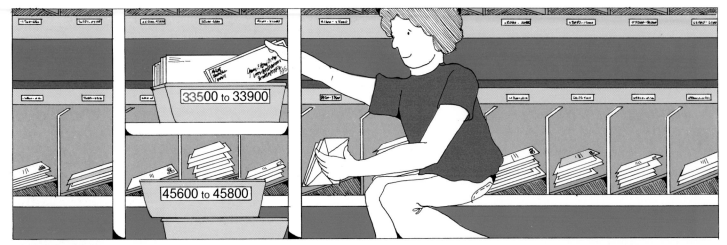

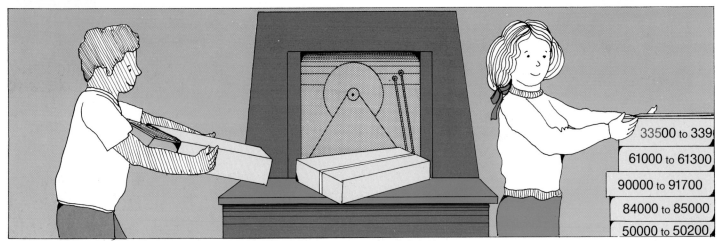

Other postal workers stack the letters into the
correct zip code trays.

The trays are then boxed and tied.

All the mail is then loaded onto trucks.

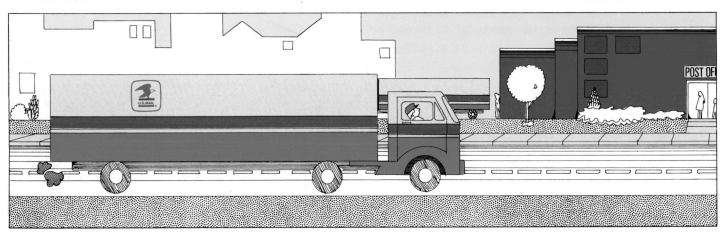

Some trucks go to boats or planes. Their mail will go to foreign countries.

Some trucks bring their zip-coded mail straight to other big area post offices.

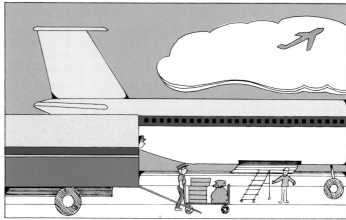
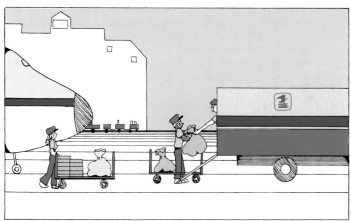

Other trucks carry zip-coded mail for faraway parts of the country. The mail is put onto planes going to the different zip code areas. There it is unloaded and sent to the correct big area post offices.

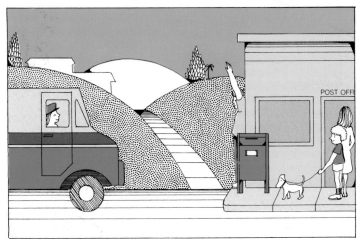

At the big area post office the mail is sorted
again to go to the smaller local post offices, where it
is sorted once more.

Some of the mail goes into private mailboxes that
people rent right at the post office.

Letter carriers pick up the rest of the mail
and deliver it

...to you.

More Mail Facts

 The word "post," as in "post office," comes to us from the days of ancient Rome. A "post" (in Latin, *positus*) was a marked place along the road where letter-carrying messengers could stop to switch their tired horses for new ones.

 In the early days of our country a letter was paid for by the person receiving it.

 George Washington, our first president, wrote the first letter to be sent by air mail. It went by balloon.

 Benjamin Franklin was the first Postmaster General of our country. His picture was on the first American postage stamp.

 The Pony Express was started in 1860 to carry mail to the new territories of the "Wild West." It took the riders 8 days to travel the rugged 1,950-mile trail.

 Camels carried mail in the South during the Civil War.

 Reindeer used to carry mail in Alaska.

 Stamp collecting is the most popular hobby in the world.

 Close to 100 billion letters and packages are mailed in the United States each year.